G]

A Poetic Précis

Ted Roberts

ARTHUR H. STOCKWELL LTD.
Torrs Park   Ilfracombe   Devon
Established 1898
www.ahstockwell.co.uk

© Ted Roberts, 2007
First published in Great Britain, 2007
All rights reserved.
No part of this publication may be reproduced
or transmitted in any form or by any means,
electronic or mechanical, including photocopy,
recording, or any information storage and
retrieval system, without permission
in writing from the copyright holder.

British Library Cataloguing-in-Publication Data.
A catalogue record for this book is available
from the British Library.

ISBN 978-0-7223-3835-3
Printed in Great Britain by
Arthur H. Stockwell Ltd.
Torrs Park   Ilfracombe
Devon

It is my hope that any who read my précis of Genesis will be prompted to turn to the Scriptures where, with careful reading, they will find that there can be no substitute for the Scriptures themselves.

I should like to express my indebtedness to the Amplified Bible, for the meaningful interpretations of place names, which I have used in this work.

My sincere thanks are also due to Philip Harrison, Betty Jones, Sylvia Hughes, Joan Neville and members of my family for the helpful encouragement which they have given me concerning my writing.

GENESIS

Ch. 1.

In the beginning God created
The heavens and the earth.
And God said, "Let there be light."
And there was light of good worth.
God had worked in the dark
Without a single spark,
Yet it must be understood
That what He made was good.

The earth was without form and void.
Other powers had to be employed.
The Spirit of God moved on the water
Stirring every lifeless quarter.
There was much to be done yet:
Everywhere was wet.

He made the clouds that float
Above the firmament of heaven:
A space which to the birds and bees
And butterflies was given.
Change in shape was near
For the soaking sphere.
God said, "Let the dry land appear."
And it did!

Then, satisfied with sea and land,
The seeds of life abroad He fanned.
Trees grew tall and herbs grew short:
Plants of every size and sort.
Sun, moon and stars were set on high,
Birds in the firmament started to fly
And beneath the water's swish
God placed shoals and schools of fish.

Land-loving creatures made He at will,
But He saved to the last His greatest thrill.
"Let us make man in our own image," said He,
And that's how humans came to be.
Though fashioned from the dust of the ground,
The vainest creatures ever found.

Ch. 2.

God rested on the seventh day
And hallowed it and blessed.
The Almighty, Source of Boundless Energy,

Appreciating rest!
This of all that's said of God
Is the hardest to be believed:
The day He honoured most
Is that on which He nought achieved.

God gave to man the breath of life;
Gave for his help a flesh-of-his-flesh wife;
Gave him rule, responsibility,
His work, the promotion of fecundity;
Gave him a garden, the fairest place on earth,
Hoping that man would understand its worth.
Alas! God's wishes were overridden
By man confronted by that which was forbidden.

Ch. 3.

At the Tree of Knowledge our parents stood
Wondering: "What is evil? What is good?"
Perplexedly pondering the question: "Why
If we choose to eat, should we have to die?"
Perhaps they had made a better choice
Had it not been for a serpent's voice
Protesting that God had told a lie,
And saying, "If you eat of that fruit you will not surely die."

The tree was good and pleasant to the eyes;
A tree to be desired to make one wise.
But, as they held in their hands the fruit freshly bitten,
They fled from their God conscience-smitten,

And while from His presence they fearfully hide,
They know in their hearts that something has died.

Sad the woman, unhappy the man
For the tale of woe which they began,
Starting a battle (which no man could win)
Against the evil of inbred sin.
Dismissed from Eden, their relationship o'er,
God and mankind were at peace no more.
Sword-wielding angels barred the way
To the Tree of Life and eternal day.

Ch. 4.

Soon our parents, Adam and Eve,
By their children are taught to grieve,
For in the wake of what they have done,
Their firstborn murders their second son:
The firstborn son of the first ever mother
Takes the life of his only brother.
God, who had witnessed Abel's death,
Had seen him draw his latest breath,
Asked Cain where his brother was?
Cain answered, "I don't know, because
I'm not my brother's keeper."

God ignored his insolence;
Told him straight to get from thence,
A fugitive to be.
"My punishment" cried Cain, "I cannot bear.

No man now my life will spare;
In vengeance all will slay me."
Upon his forehead, there and then,
God wrote a sign to warn all men
That vengeance, vengeance makes
And vengeance multiplied will be
Through him who vengeance takes.
Thus, protected by his injured God,
Cain survived in the Land of Nod.

Ch. 5.
Adam to Noah's descendants.

Chs. 6 – 9.
The Deluge.

The Sons of God, not angels but men,
Saw that the daughters of men were fair
And took them wives wherever they would;
And giants were bred here and there:
And men, now knowing evil from good,
Chose evil everywhere.
Such worldwide wantonness brought on a flood:
Universal destruction from a distraught God.

Noah's character was blameless
When all but him were shameless.
He built an ark gigantic, as directed by the Lord,
And twos and sevens of every creature he took on board.
The family of eight left it not too late,

But, while others mocked,
The ark they provisioned and stocked,
Until that day
When by rain all the smiles were washed away.

The fountains of the deep were opened,
The waters rose on high,
But higher still heaven's windows
Poured water from the sky,
Surging up and cascading down:
All outside the ark must drown.
The earth seemed back where it had started:
The waters covered the earth; they were unparted.

Over a year they floated and sailed,
So long had the flood prevailed.
A raven first flew away from the boat
And never came back:
It had found sustenance afloat.

Next to leave was a dove:
Symbol of peace and love.
No peace it found on the surface below,
Nowhere could she her love bestow.
Back into the ark she flew,
To be welcomed with "Veroo! Veroo!"
But presently once more did launch
Returning with an olive branch.
The eight inside were all elated:
Clearly the waters were abated.

At least some beasts were sorry the flood had ended,
For they soon, as offerings, in smoke ascended.
The flood would never happen again:
It had caused God too much pain.
It almost seemed He would declare,
"Their punishment is greater than I can bear."
Perhaps the implications are:
God thought that He had gone too far,
For in the sky He set His bow,
That henceforth everyone should know
The fountains would never open again;
Nevermore would there be such rain.

Now Noah was a husbandman
And gathered from the vine
The finest grapes that ever were,
And fermented such good wine
That he himself had overdrunk
And naked to his couch had sunk.
Ham called upon his sire and went,
Unexpected, into his father's tent,
Saw him lying on the floor
And told his brothers what he saw.
In doing so, he did demean their parent
In a manner quite obscene.

On waking, knowing what Ham had done,
Noah pronounced a curse upon his son:
"Canaan shall subservient be;
To his brothers a menial he!"

Prophetic words did Noah rehearse:
So much later fell the curse.

Ch. 10.
Descendants of Noah.

Ch. 11.
The Tower of Babel and Genealogy of Abram.

What was it that the Lord despised at Babel's lofty tower?
Unity? Sweet Unity, which has peace in her power?
One people occupied the earth;
One language did they speak.
'Divide to rule' some sense does make,
But does it, merely to make them weak?
Alas! for 'Unity is strength'
And by that strength was given
The arrogance to try to build a spurious way to heaven.
Man's fame, not God's, was on their mind,
Themselves they saw: to heaven were blind.

Nahor (father),
Terah (son),
Abram, Nahor and Haran (grandsons),
Dwellers in Chaldea before Terah his travels began.

Haran had passed away before the journey had started
When Terah and his sons from Chaldea for ever parted.
Six hundred miles they journeyed along Euphrates' span
And honoured the dead where they settled,

By calling the place 'Haran'.

Ch. 12.

Lissom the lakes and lovely
And sweet the rivers which at Haran flow,
But a voice insisted,
"Abram, it is elsewhere you must go.
You must go to a land which I shall show you,
Where your descendents for ever shall live:
A land which flows with milk
And where the bees rich honey give.
And I" said God, "will bless you
And great shall be your name.
As the sand of the sea your seed shall be,
As the stars widespread your fame.
And you shall be a blessing
In the land of your possessing,
And north and south and east and west
In you and in your seed
Shall all the families of the earth be blessed."
Abram took his wife, Sarai, and Lot, dead Haran's son,
A comfort to the couple, for children they had none.

Abram, Sarai and Lot left Haran:
The pleasant spot, of which they had never tired,
Taking with them riches which they had there acquired.
Trusting God, the faithful band entered into Canaan's land.
But the Land of Milk and Honey knew a time of drought,
And famine, cruel and severe, drove the settlers out.

In search of sustenance, in Egypt they arrived,
To find that while Canaan suffered
The realm of the pharaohs thrived.

Abram looked at Sarai and feared for his life;
"Tell them you're my sister," he said.
"Don't let them know you're my wife."
Sarai, whose beauty turned all men's heads her way,
Agreed to the deception, lest they should her husband slay.

To Pharaoh's harem she was brought,
But before he could her take,
God sorely plagued the land of Egypt, all for Sarai's sake.
Pharaoh questioned Abram: "Why have you me misled?"
Abram bowed to Pharaoh. "I was afraid," he said.
Then Pharaoh ordered Abram, "Depart from my domain.
Take your possessions with you
And don't come back again."

Ch. 13.

Wealthier than when they left, to Canaan they returned,
To find that verdure filled the land
Which once was dead and burned.

So little distance had they gone
Before they found they could not go on:
Abram and his late brother's son travelling together.
Quarrels came as went the days:
About whose flocks here or there should graze;

To which flock belonged which water?
Questions and arguments in every quarter,
Until the parents (surrogate)
From their nephew separate.

When Abram, with kindly voice,
Offered to Lot the right of choice,
Lot found it easy to make up his mind.
The watery plains of Jordan were easy to find.
Travelling to the east his herdsmen made their way;
To the west of the River Jordan's banks Abram's future lay.

Ch. 14.
Lot Is Taken Prisoner.

Lot settled at Sodom, seemingly secure,
But his dependence on Abram was far from o'er.
Plundering kings of Shinar Jordan's plain invaded.
Lot, his family and his wealth were taken as they raided.

Shinar's fearsome four Jordan's five kings defeated,
But they had not reckoned with Abram,
As homeward they retreated.
Where did Abram learn such skill
His friends and servants so to drill,
That with the friendly Amorite,
Striking in the dead of night,
They should the four of Shinar slay
And victorious bring away

The rescued prisoners and the spoil,
Restoring them to Jordan's soil?
The hero of this story
Himself to God gave all the glory.
"From the Lord" said Abram, "comes all my success:
All that I've achieved and all that I possess."

Ch. 15.

"Though very old," said Abram, "still I believe
Sarai (as God promised) will my child conceive."
God honoured Abram's faith confessed:
"Counted it to him as righteousness,"
And in visions of the night
Told of Israel's future bright,
But that Abram's seed must see
Four hundred years of slavery
Before (when from thraldom they have fled)
To the Promised Land being led.

Ch. 16.

Sarai had not Abram's faith.
The promise caused her mirth.
She laughed to scorn the whole idea saying,
"At my age, giving birth!
Come, Abram, take my handmaid as your concubine;
The bearing shall be hers, the motherhood be mine."

Handmaiden Hagar conceived a child.
Sarai was ashamed.

Her disappointment she could not hide,
But it was Abram she blamed.
"She's just a servant," Abram said,
"Sarai, you're my wife!
You may deal with her just as you please;
Make miserable her life."
This dictum from her noble lord, Sarai took so literally
That Hagar to the wilderness fled from such cruelty.

At the fountain of Shur, Hagar's sorrow turned to joy
On learning that her child would be a princely baby boy.
The Lord himself from heaven appeared
To tell her, "Ishmael, your son, will not die.
Put away your sore distress;
Go back and serve your old mistress
And Ishmael shall grow up to be
A mighty man of destiny."

Ch. 17.

God's words concerning Ishmael to Abram He retold:
He would become a prince of men, fearless and bold.
Sarai's son, though not yet conceived,
The name of Isaac then received.
Abram, renamed Abraham*, at this point was advised
That all his sons, his serfs, and his slaves
Must be circumcised,
And God covenanted with him to bless
This rite of health and righteousness.

Father of a Multitude.

Ch.18.

Three men visited Abraham. They stood at his tent door.
They washed, they dined and rested,
Then told what lay in store.
For Sodom, sinful Sodom, wracked by debauchery,
Would soon in judgement lie buried
Beneath the salt Dead Sea.
"Supposing fifty righteous should in the city dwell?
Forty-five? Forty? Thirty? Twenty? Ten?
Should they all die as well?"
Abraham put the questions.
God's answer was more than fair:
"If I ten righteous find therein, I will the city spare."
Why did Abraham not go on?
Would God have spared the city for one?
Abraham, in truth, knew not
What in Sodom had become of Lot.
Had he stood firm or been dragged down
By pervasive iniquity in the town?

Ch. 19.

At evening Lot sat by Sodom's gate.
Two angels* entered, to whom Lot said, "The hour is late.
It is not safe the streets to roam.
Come with me! Come with me to my home."
Lot, his daughters and his spouse,

*Angels having the appearance of men.

From the angels, in the house,
Heard of the imminent destruction,
And from the angels took instruction:
They to the mountains now must fly,
For to remain in Sodom would be to die.

To his married daughters and sons-in-law
Straightway Lot made his way.
They heard from him of the angels' warning,
Heard all he had to say.
But, though they could see how deeply he was shocked,
To them, 'he seemed as one that mocked;'
Seemed as one too easily deceived;
Seemed the warning too readily to have believed.
They, themselves, in Sodom would remain,
Taking their chance on Jordan's plain.
Home again, the anxious four
Themselves for flight prepare,
When bangs upon the door are heard
And screamed demanding fills the outside air:
"Those men so fair you have in there;
Send them out! Show them!
Such lovely looks! Such fine physiques!
We want to know them!"

Lot stepped outside to face the crowd,
Offering them a choice,
And through the uproar, ever loud,
He made them hear his voice:
"Take my virgin daughters," he cried.

"Leave these men alone!
Do not the wickedness you plan."
The crowd impatient moan.
"My daughters or no one!" cried Lot.
The crowd refuses to budge
And cries; "You're just a stranger here.
Who made you our judge?
Give us the men! The men! The men!
Or suffer for their sake.
If you do not give them up,
Yours is the body we'll take."

Strong the hands which opened the door
And drew Lot into the house;
Mighty the men who faced the crowd
His cause to espouse;
Angelic the eyes which scanned the crowd
One righteous soul to find;
Divine the power which judged them all
And struck the rapists blind.
"It's time to go," the angels said;
"Delay not in all the plain.
To the mountains you must haste away
Some time there to remain,
But, as you follow the ascending track,
Take care that none of you look back."

On the plain of Jordan they spent yet one night more.
The angels giving permission
Spared the little town of Zoar,

But dawn's first light had scarcely shone
Before from Zoar the group had gone.
Sadly, on that historic morning,
As to the mountains they covered the ground,
Lot's wife ignored the angels' warning
And, taking one last look at Sodom, turned herself around.
Was it forgetfulness? Or was she recklessly at fault,
That she, a wife and mother, should be turned to salt?

Oh, virgin daughters, what possessed you
That for progeny's sake
You should intoxicate your father
And him as husband take?
No other husbands could you find
And so you thought it best,
But foes of Abraham's seed you spawned
In your vile incest.

Ch. 20.

When Abraham went from Egypt,
Eastwards to Caanan's south,
The lie, which fooled a pharaoh,
Was again in Abraham's mouth.
Abimelech, King of Gerar, took Sarah as a wife,
But God warned him in a dream,
"Touch her and I'll end your life."
The king his innocence protested,
God respected his plea;
The next day, unmolested, Sarah again was free.

With God's protection ever near,
How strange that Abraham felt such fear!
Believing no pagan could resist her,
All were told, "She is my sister."
Loaded with wealth, from Egypt,
Abraham was forced to roam,
But Abimelech, the Philistine, gave him gifts
And offered him a home.

Ch. 21.

Sarah conceived and bore a son.
What God had promised He had done.
Sarah's sceptical laughter
Had turned to peals of joy,
For feeding at her bosom was Isaac,
Her own baby boy.

Ishmael couldn't behave himself.
He poked fun at his infant brother,
Which didn't bother Abraham,
But it really riled his mother.

Perhaps it's natural in any lad
To make fun of the son
Of a ninety-year-old mother
And a one-hundred-year-old dad.

Abraham loved his son, Ishmael,
But his wife got on to him so

That it's back to the wilderness
Hagar and her son must go.

Ishmael came close to death
When their water bottle ran dry,
But the angel of God rescued Hagar and him,
When He showed them a well nearby.
Ishmael became a great hunter,
Took an Egyptian lady to wife,
Founded a nation and mourned, with Isaac,
At the end of their father's life.

Abimelech with Phichol, the chief captain of his host,
Called upon Abraham about the two things he feared most.
After Abraham's deception concerning Sarah,
Abimelech was wary of Abraham's guile
And he was aware that, whatever Abraham did,
Upon him God would smile.
Fearing God and afraid of God's man,
Abimelech came with a friendship plan:
"The kindness I have shown you of late,
Swear that to me and mine you will reciprocate."
Why did Abimelech take with him Phichol,
Who was clearly a man of war?
Could it be that he wanted Abraham
To think about what he saw?
"Your men have driven me from my well," said Abraham;
"About this I must complain."
"I knew not of it," claimed Abimelech;
"You shall have it back again."

Ch. 22.

Abraham, by God, was sent to the land of Moriah,
There to build an altar and on it to light a fire
And make a sacrifice thereon
Of beloved Isaac, his only son.
Prior to ignition Abraham raised a knife
With which to end for ever Isaac's precious life,
But a voice from heaven cried, "Harm not the lad!"
Sufficient proof of Abraham's faith the Lord already had.

Yet a sacrifice to the Lord was brought:
A ram by the horns in a thicket caught.
The angel called a second time and God swore by Himself
That Abraham's seed as the stars should be
And as countless as the sand of the sea.
His power over his foes was to be immense
Because of his faith and obedience.

Ch. 23.

One hundred and twenty-seven
Were the years of Sarah's life.
In all his grief Abraham needed to own
The burial place of his late wife.
Ephron the Hittite offered for free
The land Abraham wanted most,
But Abraham could not allow him
To the Hebrew dead to play host.
Nor could he, as he was offered,

A distinguished grave with Hittites share:
His dead were not to lie at the sites
Where were practised pagan rites.

Ch. 24.

Now Nahor's son, Bethuel,
Whose mother's name was Milcah,
Had a lovely daughter whom he named Rebekah.
On hearing of Rebekah it entered Abraham's head
That his beautiful great niece should Isaacwards be led.
He would have gone and fetched the lass
From the land where she was bred,
But he felt far too old to go
And sent his most trustworthy servant
To woo the girl instead.
The servant was a religious man,
Who did his duty religiously,
And brought Rebekah Isaacwards
With the utmost celerity.

When Isaac saw Rebekah, she took away his breath.
Immediately he loved her
And was comforted after his mother's death.

Ch. 25.

Abraham married Keturah, who bore him many a son.
On maturity Abraham gave them gifts
And sent them away to settle east of the Jordan.

Ishmael had twelve sons, who princes all became,
Each with a castle, town and nation bearing his name.
A good relationship may have developed
Between Isaac and Ishmael,
For they were together to honour their father at his burial.

Rebekah longed for twenty years
For the day when she a child would bear.
Then Esau* and Jacob† she conceived
In answer to Isaac's prayer.
She was puzzled to find that, in her womb,
Twins, with each other, made affray.
God told her their lives would be contentious
And the younger over the elder would hold sway.

Esau was born looking like a garment,
From head to feet covered in red hair.
Jacob was born a plain child
Whose skin was smooth and fair.
These Isaac's only children ever would remain,
For his only wife, Rebekah, never bore again.
Esau, first into the world, did steal,
With Jacob holding him by the heel.
Esau became a hunter; in the fields his life was spent.
Jacob lived more conventionally,
Preferring the comfort of a tent.
Isaac loved Esau for the venison on which he fed,

*Esau = Hairy.
†Jacob = Supplanter.

Rebekah favoured Jacob for the kind of life he led.
Differences between them unfolded one by one,
Until the elder, for soup and a piece of bread,
Would sell his birthright to the younger son.

Ch. 26.

When famine returned to the Promised Land,
Isaac to Gerar went,
By God's command avoiding Egypt,
To which his father had been sent.
Isaac, like his father before him, feared for his life.
Rebekah, like Sarah before her,
Was obliged to pretend she wasn't his wife.

The Philistine king kept his eye on them
And from his window peering about
Caught the couple canoodling and found the fibbing out.
Abimelech could scarce believe what he saw
And, feeling his anger mount,
Summoned Isaac to appear before him,
Calling him to account.
From the Scriptures it would appear
That no explanation could Isaac frame.
Perhaps he stood like a naughty boy
And hung his head in shame.
From Gerar, Isaac was ordered away
And in moving not to dally;
In fact, he hardly moved at all:
He set himself up in Gerar Valley.

Why had the Philistines filled in the wells
By Abraham excavated?
Did they fear that strangers would settle around them?
Was this a prospect they hated?
Two wells of his father's Isaac reopened
Only for the Philistines to drive him away;
But a third he reopened and they gave up –
Isaac was there to stay,
Until, the famine over, he returned to the land
Which for him, by God, was meant.
There he built an altar to the Lord
And firmly pitched his tent.
Then he re-dug the well which his father had dug
And had given it Beer-she-ba as its name:
'The Well of the Oath' was its meaning
And Isaac called it the same.

Esau typically took to himself
Two Canaanite wives in marriage:
Unions which his parents were vehemently to disparage.

Ch. 27.

The struggles in the womb's forebodings
Came to fruition by a wise mother's goadings.
That Isaac's final blessing
With the birthright essentially must go
Was something which both of the parents
Most certainly would know.
Rebekah persuaded Jacob his father to deceive;

Thus, clad in furs and Esau's clothes,
That he was Esau, Jacob made his father believe.
Isaac being aged and blind, Jacob and Rebekah knew
That Esau, who sold his birthright for soup,
Would gladly buy the vital blessing
With a bowl of venison stew.

Esau, on pleading, received a blessing,
But not that of the firstborn.
He felt cheated, angry, rejected
And deeply, so deeply forlorn.
"I'll kill him!" he said, perhaps to his friends,
Not knowing that his mother
Of his intentions would hear.
Rebekah knew that he meant what he said
And was overcome with fear.
"Jacob," she said, "you must leave here,
Until Esau's anger turns away,
For your brother intends to kill you.
Why should I lose you both in one day?"

Rebekah spoke to Isaac
About the wives of Esau's choice.
About her concern for Jacob
She movingly raised her voice:
"What good shall my life do me
If Jacob should a Canaanite take?"
Isaac knew, as she spoke,
That to Haran, Jacob his way must make.

Ch. 28.

Isaac summoned Jacob and told him,
"Take not a wife from the daughters of Canaan.
Go to Padan-ar-am.
Take a wife from the daughters of Laban."
Then he blessed him as God's chosen man.
Esau, hearing this blessing,
Understood he had married amiss
And, taking two wives from the daughters of Ishmael,
Thought he would his errors redress.
But he had two more mistakes to repine,
For his new wives were of the wrong Abrahamic line.

Jacob journeyed until the sun with its light had fled.
In the darkness he gathered smooth stones
And made of them a bed.
As he lay down, perhaps he hoped
In a dream his future wife to see:
A wife with whom he could happily share
The divinely promised prosperity.
Dream he did, but of a ladder
From earth to heaven extended,
On the rungs of which the angels of God
Ascended and descended.
God at the top of the ladder stood,
Giving to Jacob tidings good:
God's promises to his fathers he was to inherit.
All that Esau had forfeited was given to him on merit.

Jacob awoke from sleep believing he was
At God's dwelling place.
He was filled with dread and God's kindly words
Could not his fears efface.
He transformed his pillows into a pillar;
An offering of oil he made;
Renamed the place Bethel*
And thus his fears he allayed.
Before leaving Bethel he made a vow:
"My Protector shall my God be now."

Ch. 29.

Jacob at Haran safely arrived:
Haran, where flocks grazed well and thrived.
The well at Haran was sealed with a stone:
A rock not easily moved by one man alone.
Quaintly Jacob asked them, "Whence be ye?"
Rhymingly they answered, "Of Haran are we."
"Do you know Laban?" he inquired. "Is he well?"
"We know him; he's healthy," they were happy to tell,
Adding, "Here comes Rachel, his daughter,
Bringing his flock."
When Jacob heard this it almost seems as if he
Went into shock.
He requested the shepherds their flocks to water
And go and leave him with Laban's daughter.
When Rachel arrived, Jacob shifted the stone
And watered the sheep all on his own.

*Bethel = The House of God.

Jacob introduced himself with tears, a kiss and a sigh.
Rachel ran to tell her father, leaving Jacob with no reply.
Laban ran to greet him,
Embraced him and kissed his cheek,
Then took him to his home, all his news to seek.
For seven years Jacob worked for Laban,
Rachel for his wife to earn;
But, concerning Laban, Jacob had a lot to learn.

On Jacob's wedding night, Laban brought him Leah,
And in the darkness Jacob was deceived,
Simply because he could not see her.
When Jacob complained, Laban craftily said,
"In this country, the firstborn
Before the second must wed."
Jacob worked for Rachel another seven years;
It may be hoped he bought his wives by paying in arrears.
Because Leah, the lonely, unchosen bride
Coveted Jacob's love for Rachel,
(Love which he made no attempt to hide)
God pitied the neglected one:
Enabled her to have Reuben,
Jacob's firstborn son.
Reuben's birth gave Leah the hope
That now Jacob would love her and adore,
But Jacob's heart was Rachel's
And remained so evermore.

Leah was thankful to the Lord.
She knew her prayers He had been hearing.
Three more sons she bore for Jacob
Before, for a while, she left off bearing.

Ch. 30.

Rachel enviously accosted Jacob:
"Give me children or I die!"
Angrily Jacob rounded on her:
"Do you think that God am I?
Should God's withholding the fruit of your womb
Cause you to crave an early tomb?"
"Then take my maid, Bilhah," cried Rachel,
"And, if it God should please,
She shall have my children;
She shall bear them upon my knees."

Bilhah produced Dan and Naphtali;
Leah regarded them with jealous eye.
The battle was on! It was tit for tat!
She too had a maid and thought, 'I can do that.'
Leah's maid, Zilpah, had yet another lad:
"A troop comes," Leah prophesied
And therefore named him Gad*.

Zilpah equalled Bilhah when her second son came.
"I shall be blessed among women!" she said,
"Asher† shall be his name."
Her eldest son, at harvest time,
Found mandrakes in a wheat field.
Though they were not purposely planted,
Great would be their yield.

*Gad = Fortune.
†Asher = Happy.

"Let me have some of your mandrakes,"
Rachel requested Leah.
(Those fertility symbols, those gifts from her son,
Reuben's mother held dear.)
"You have taken my man," she retorted;
"Would you take my mandrakes too?
These gifts from my son are precious to me;
Do you think I would give them to you?"

Rachel paid for the mandrakes
In a way which does not seem nice:
She hired out Jacob to Leah:
One night in bed was the price.
But Leah received more than one night of pleasure.
Hers was joy beyond all measure.
Issachar was born to her
And she with Jacob did not leave it there.
Issachar was her fifth, but not her final son,
For he was followed by Zebulun.
And more time spent with Jacob brought her
Dinah! A girl! Jacob's only daughter!

God remembered, and listened to Rachel
And as His response
Rachel gave birth to Joseph,
The wisest and most righteous of all of Jacob's sons.
It must be that God had informed her
She would have one other child: a boy.
As she considered His promise,
Was sadness mingled in her joy?

Jacob appealed to Laban: "Send me now away
To my own country, in my own place to stay.
Let me take my wives and children,
Which, from you, I have earned;
Let me seek prosperity in the land
For which I have yearned.
How well I have served you I'm sure you know.
It's time now for me to set up on my own.
I pray you, Laban, let me go."

"If I," said Laban, "have found favour in your eyes,
I pray you, stay a while longer with me.
That the Lord blesses me for your sake I can plainly see.
You can name your own wages,
For, without your skill and drive,
I am aware my fortunes will suffer.
Without you, I know, I cannot thrive.
What shall I give you?" cried Laban.
"You shall give me nothing," Jacob replied.
"What I take from you I again shall earn."
Then Jacob made Laban an offer
Which the Syrian could not spurn:
"Let me have the spotted and speckled goats,
And let me take all the brown sheep.
And all the white beasts, when I take my leave,
Shall be yours, Laban, to keep."

With the help of God and some peeled stripy sticks,
On the healthiest and best of Laban's white flock
Jacob worked some wonderful tricks.

In their watering troughs
Before their eyes the sticks were set,
So that spotted and speckled
Were the lambs they would get.
Those fine, healthy lambs were taken away,
After a three-day journey, with Jacob's sons to stay.
The weaker white lambs, with Jacob left behind,
Were all that Laban, as his, would find.

Ch. 31.

It is hardly any wonder that Laban had a shock
When at length he came to see the condition of his flock.
The disappointment showed in his face
And anger as clear as could be.
The change in his attitude towards himself,
Jacob could plainly see.
Laban's sons too were heard to say,
"All that our father had, Jacob has taken away."
However, in everything that he had done,
The guidance of God, Jacob had known.
Time and again, concerning his wages,
By Laban, Jacob had been deceived.
Now, by God's directing and Jacob's labours,
Retribution Laban received.

For confrontation with Laban, Jacob had little heart.
And Laban had lost the respect of his daughters,
Who were happy from him to part.
Jacob sent for his wives to meet him

Where he was working in the field.
There, all their grievances against Laban
They to each other revealed.
With each other they commiserated.
Oh, how low they justly Laban rated!

Jacob, his wives and all his sons
Considered Laban incurably bent.
They gathered their flocks, loaded their camels
And on their way they went.
Three days passed before Laban heard
That Jacob and all that was his had gone.
He gathered his brethren behind him
And the race to catch Jacob was on.
His pursuers overtook him at Mount Gilead.
There, by God in a dream, Laban was warned:
"Neither promise Jacob good; nor threaten him with bad."

"What have you done?" he asked Jacob,
"Stealing away without a word,
Carrying off my daughters
As though you had won them by your sword.
We could have celebrated with music,
With laughter and with song,
But not a kiss from my sons or my daughters!
Why have you done me this wrong?
It is in my power to punish you,
But your God, in my dreams, said to me
That I must contain my anger; I must let you be.

But one issue I will take up with you:
You have your great God, to whom you pray,
So tell me, why did you steal my idols
On the night you stole away?"

Jacob answered, "I was afraid
You would take your daughters from me by force.
If anyone here has your idols,
Let him be slain, as a matter of course."
In believing that all were innocent,
Jacob was mistaken,
For Rachel, the wife he idolised,
Had her father's idols taken.
Laban searched every tent and saddle,
But was never to see his idols again,
For Rachel, sitting over the idols,
Made excuse in her saddle to remain:
"Let it not displease my lord,
In that I cannot rise up before thee.
Embarrass me not, I beseech you,
For the custom of women is upon me."

Laban's search ended. Nothing had he found.
Jacob was angry – angry enough on Laban to round.
"Why have you pursued me?
What is my trespass? What is my sin?
What stolen have you found in my tents
Or my baggage within?
Twenty years I served you, in days of drought
And cruel nights of frost.

Stock, by thieves, was stolen!
Predators tore and devoured them!
And always, **always, always, I bore the cost.**
You have no idea how little I slept,
As over your flocks and mine a constant vigil I kept.
If my God, in your dreams,
Had not rebuked you last night,
You would have sent me away,
With little as my pay.
That would have been my plight."

Laban was a mean man:
His own daughters of money he had deprived.
They would have been happy to see him go
As quickly as he had arrived.
Laban answered Jacob in somewhat altered style,
As all that Jacob had taken
Passed through his mind in file:
"These daughters, these children, these cattle,
All the things you see are mine.
What could I do to my daughters?
What could I do to their young?"
Laban's feigning must have sounded to Jacob
Like a bad song, badly sung.

Before parting, Laban suggested
That a verbal covenant they make,
But Jacob at once decided a stone for a pillar to take.
Then, with many smaller stones,
A pile as a platform he laid,
And thereupon, with his sons, they dined

And vows of non-aggression made.
The stones were to be a witness
To the vows they ought never rescind.
Verbal vows can be forgotten,
Like the breath on which they are uttered,
Dispersed with the wind.
"These stones shall be our witness," Laban said,
But it was from the work of Jacob and his sons
That the thought had entered his head.

Laban called the pile Jegarsahadutha*;
Jacob named it Galeed†.
"This pillar and pile which I have set," said Laban,
"Shall be witnesses of which God shall take good heed.
He shall judge between us for so long as we are apart,
Should you afflict my daughters,
Or other wives take to your heart."
How carefully did Laban his every word choose,
For he would have murdered Jacob
Could he have found an excuse.
Therefore he named the pile Mizpah‡:
A name implying a threat,
For, in his heart, Laban hoped
That he would vanquish Jacob yet.
Laban did so much talking,
But it was Jacob who set the scene;
Laban who spoke of avoiding harm,
But Jacob who planned for a future serene.

*Jegarsahadutha: = 'Witness Heap' in Aramaic.
†Galeed: = 'Witness Heap' in Hebrew.
‡Mizpah: = 'Watchpost' (implying mistrust).

It was Jacob who brought bread,
That, on the pile, the meal of friendship
Should take place;
Laban who kissed and embraced
His daughters and grandsons,
But placed no kiss on Jacob's face.

Ch. 32.

Jacob continued his journeying
To the promised south.
Again he received encouragement
Proceeding from angelic mouth.
Mehanaim* he named the place where he the angels met,
But thoughts of meeting Esau caused him to fear and fret.
Messengers he sent to Esau to herald his approach,
For soon on Esau's territory he needs must encroach.

The messengers returning
Brought alarm to Jacob's group,
For they told of Esau's coming towards them,
Leading a four-hundred-man troop.
In spite of God's promised protection,
He divided his folk and flocks into two,
That if one group attacked should be,
The other would have a chance to flee.

He confessed his unworthiness of all God's help
In yielding to fear of what his brother might do.

**Mehanaim = Two Armies.*

41

When, by anxiety driven,
He had divided his party into two,
Ten miles to the River Jabbok he retreated,
Sent his wives and eleven sons across its ford,
Then turned to the south, alone to face
The ever advancing Edomite lord.
Jacob sent gifts of droves of beasts,
To greet Esau on the way.
When "Whose are these?" Esau enquired,
"Gifts of appeasement from your servant,"
Was all the drovers were to say.

While waiting south of the Jabbok,
There came to Jacob a man,
Who, with strength and skill, wrestled him
Through the hours of darkness' span.
As daylight broke, the mysterious man
Over Jacob had not prevailed.
Jacob's skill had not let him down,
Nor had his strength or courage failed,
But the man, in the hollow of Jacob's thigh,
Touched a vital point:
A sinew shrank and, for the rest of his life,
Jacob's thigh was out of joint.
The man then said to Jacob, "Let me go."
Jacob firmly answered, "Until you bless me, no!"
On being asked, Jacob told the man his name.
"From now on your name shall be Israel*,"
Back the answer came.

Israel = Contender with God.

"For as a prince you have not failed;
With God and man you have prevailed."
Then Jacob dared to ask the name
Of him who had wrestled and made him lame.
"Why do you ask it?" the man replied.
Jacob knew his request was out of place,
For he knew who it was and cried,
"I have seen God face to face!"
Then he gave the name Penuel*
To the venue of the duel.

Ch. 33.

At Esau and Jacob's meeting;
What an occasion! What a greeting!
They embraced, they hugged, they wept, they kissed,
Perhaps realising what, as brothers, they had missed.

Esau, protesting, accepted the gifts
Which Jacob whole-heartedly proffered.
An invitation and escort to the land of Edom
Esau then generously offered.
But the slow pace of Jacob's party's travel to match
Esau's men would difficult find,
And giving no offence to Esau
Politely Jacob the escort declined,
Promising that, in the land of Seir,
He and his party would visit Esau there.

Penuel (or Peniel) = The Face of God.

First Jacob crossed the Jordan, recuperation to find.
A house he built for his family
And booths for his livestock of every kind.
He named the place Succoth*,
And there they were blessed
With a time of recovery, leisure and rest.

Ch. 34.

Then to Shechem city they made their way:
A move for which Jacob was, for ever, to rue the day.
Simeon and Levi each took it into their head
To murder Shechem's menfolk,
For their crown prince had taken
Dinah, unwedded, to bed!

To pacify the sons of Jacob
The Shechemites, to a man,
Had agreed to be circumcised:
To become Hebrews was the plan.
But, the circumcision effected,
While each Shechemite was in pain,
Jacob's sons attacked them
And everyone from king to commoner
Was unmercifully slain.
Hamor, the king, and his son, named Shechem,
Had sought for their nation
With the Hebrews complete integration,
But while Shechem's adult men all lost their lives,
Total integration was forced
On their children and their wives.

**Succoth = Booths.*

Dinah, Jacob's only daughter, is hardly heard of again.
Was she obliged, for as long as she lived,
A spinster to remain?
Did she mourn for the rest of her life,
The prince who had loved her dearly
And would gladly have made her his wife?
How did Jacob feel about all this?
What did the patriarch think?
The answer is clear in his words to his sons:
"YOU HAVE MADE MY NAME TO STINK!
The Canaanites and Perizzites will slay me;" he cried,
"Me and all my house!"
"Should he deal with our sister as with a harlot?"
Still was his sons' feeble grouse.

Ch. 35.

Once more Jacob was assailed by fear and doubt.
Once more God spoke, telling him
That from Shechem he must move out.
Back, to where with God he began, he must now return,
For he and his erring children had such a lot to learn.

On Jacob's orders, his children
Cleared idols and earrings from every tent;
They washed themselves and put on clean clothing
Before on their way to Bethel they went.
The Canaanites and Perizzites
From vengeance were restrained;
The God who had quieted Pharaoh,
Abimelech and Laban,
Abraham's seed's Protector then, as before, remained.
At Bethel, Jacob built a new altar,

His mother's nurse reached the end of her life
And, on the way from Bethel to Ephrath,
After her giving birth to Benjamin,
Jacob lost his most loved wife.
How ironic that in days gone by,
Rachel had pleaded with Jacob,
"Give me children, or I'll die!"

After all his sufferings,
Into which, by kinsmen, he had so often been led,
What must have been Jacob's agony
On discovering his son, Reuben,
With Bilhah, his concubine,
Had defiled his father's bed?

At one hundred and eighty,
Isaac yielded up the ghost and died.
As Esau and Jacob buried him,
We may think they stood side by side
And, on parting, offered comfort
Which neither could resist.
It may be that, once again,
They embraced, hugged and kissed.

Ch. 36.
The Descendants of Esau.

Ch. 37.

Rachel, who from the day they met
Had been Jacob's most loved one,
Had (it seems not surprisingly)
Given him Joseph, his best-loved son.

As such, a coat of many colours
Marked young Joseph out:
A fact his ten elder brothers
Were not at all happy about.
In fact his brothers' resentment was extremely deep
And Joseph only made things worse
By telling of dreams, which he'd had in his sleep:
"We were binding sheaves in the field," said he;
"And your sheaves all bowed to one made by me,
And the sun and the moon and eleven stars
To me obeisance made."
Of what his brothers made of this
Joseph appeared unafraid.
Even his father rebuked him saying,
"Do you think it's true?
Shall I, your mother and your brothers all
Bow down to you?"

Nevertheless, of Joseph's words, Jacob took full stock,
But was unprepared for what happened
When Joseph went to visit his brothers
As they tended the family's flock:
"Let's slay the dreamer," they murmured,
"Drop his body into a pit.
And we'll see what becomes of his dreaming,
When we make an end of it."

Reuben, the infamous adulterer,
Shrank from such murder alarmed,
And planned to deliver Joseph
Back to his father unharmed.
"Shed not his blood," he said to his brothers,

"Thrown alive down a pit I expect
Cold, hunger, thirst and weariness
Will have the desired effect."
They took Joseph's coat from off him,
Put him in a pit which was nigh,
Then changed their minds in Reuben's absence,
When slave traders came passing by.

Twenty pieces of silver
Was all the slave traders would pay,
And, immediately, a captive to Egypt,
Joseph was on his way.
When Reuben discovered that Joseph was gone,
He tore his every garment:
"How can I face my father?" he cried,
"I whom my brother no harm meant."

In order to face their father,
They thought up a plan to deceive.
It was a plan so simple, so credible,
Which Jacob had to believe.
They took the blood of a goat,
With which they stained Joseph's coat.
When Jacob saw it, his clothes he rent
And into deepest mourning went,
Believing his son was now deceased
Having been devoured by an evil, wild beast.
In Egypt, Joseph was sold to Potiphar,
A captain of Pharaoh's guard,
And truth to tell, in Potiphar's house
Life was not at all hard.

Ch. 38.

Judah, at that time, paid a visit to a friend named Hirah,
And there he met a Canaanite woman
Of whom he became an admirer.
We are not to know her name,
But Judah fell in love with her,
Which quite him overcame.
They had three sons:
Er, Onan and Shelah they were called.
Sad to say, when they grew up,
Judah's happiness stalled.

Judah found Er a wife, whose name was Tamar,
But God slew childless Er for erring too far.
Judah made Onan give seed for his brother,
But, knowing the children would not be his,
He didn't want to bother,
And when to pass his seed the moment came around,
Onan defied his father
By spilling his seed upon the ground.
Again the wrath of God came on
And Judah lost his second son.

Judah, having lost two sons,
Refrained from risking Shelah,
And it's more than likely that the frightened young man
Had not the slightest wish to see her.
Therefore Tamar devised a way,
A trap for Er's father, Judah, to lay.

Disguised as a prostitute, she would sit
Where Judah would surely take heed.
Thus, by seducing her father-in-law,
He would supply her motherhood need.

He was newly a widower, needing comfort;
On his emotions she skilfully played.
When he asked her, "May I come in unto you?"
She asked him, "How shall I be paid?"
"I'll send you a kid from my flock," he said.
Then the bargaining took a sharp edge.
"Your promise will not be enough," she replied;
"What will you leave as a pledge?"
She asked for his staff, his bracelets and ring,
For she knew she would need each eloquent thing.
Need them she did!
Her sin could not be hid.

The man who'd supplied the fruit of her womb,
Hearing of her harlotry,
Condemned her to a fiery doom,
Until his pledges she produced,
Saying, "The man whose these are is the man I seduced.
I trapped you neither for profit nor lust.
I sought only for treatment fair and just."
Judah acknowledged the items in answer to her cry
And spared her life by saying,
"She has been more righteous than I."

In her womb, Tamar carried twins;
Pharez the title: elder brother wins,
Though the hand of Zarah first,
From the womb appeared.
Past him into the world unstoppable Pharez careered.
Red ribbon is tied around Zarah's wrist.
But the story has a prophetic twist,
For God to Pharez would afford
A place in the ancestry of the Lord.

Ch. 39.

Potiphar prospered because of Joseph.
He put Joseph in charge of all he had,
But Potiphar's wife longed for Joseph,
Would have had him indulge her passions bad.
Pestering him, her longings out of control,
She tore the coat from the noble soul.
He fled, having her overtures refused,
To find that of the evil she had planned
He then stood accused.

Potiphar believed her story
And made a prompt decision
That Joseph should incarcerated be
In Pharaoh's special prison,
Where Joseph soon found himself in charge
Of prison affairs both by and at large.

Ch. 40.

A butler and a baker there asked him
To interpret their dreams.
Joseph gave them God's answers,
Which were of two extremes:
The butler was to be restored to his former place;
The baker, alas! was to be hanged.
For him there would be no such grace.

Ch. 41.

Two more years Joseph was to languish,
Not without some feelings of anguish,
In Pharaoh's prison,
Until the pharaoh had dreams,
Which were meaningful, he was sure.
It was only then that the butler
Remembered the prisoner, Joseph, once more.
He told of the dreams which had been explained,
And no longer in prison Joseph remained.

Pharaoh called him before his throne
To tell of the dreams he'd had of his own:
"I dreamt seven fat cows came out of a river,
Followed by seven weak and thin.
The thin cows ate up the fat ones.
To understand the dream, how do I begin?
I dreamt too that seven ears of corn
Came up on a stalk, strong and good,
To be eaten by seven weaker ears.
How can this be understood?"

"Mighty Pharaoh!" Joseph answered,
"God has shown you what He is about to do.
The meaning of the dream He has given to me,
That I may convey it to you.
Your two dreams are as one.
Seven years of plenty are presently coming on.
These will be followed by seven years of drought.
Store the nation's food in the good years,
That in the bad years it will not run out."

To Joseph, who had managed a house
And a prison too,
Pharaoh said, "Now rule my land;
That's what you must do."

The first seven years under Joseph
The Egyptians stored their corn,
So that, in the years of famine,
None with hunger were forlorn.

Ch. 42.

Other nations sent to Egypt precious corn to buy;
Inevitably came the day,
When Joseph's brothers drew nigh.
Joseph's prophecy coming true,
Because of the scale of the dearth,
His elder brothers bowed down to him,
Their faces to the earth.
They began to think that the mighty man
Would make them victims of his whim,
For, though Joseph knew his brothers,
They did not recognise him.

Joseph accused his brethren, saying they were spies.
They told him of Jacob and Benjamin,
But he answered, "You're telling lies."
He decided to keep Simeon hostage,
While the rest took home precious grain,
And he said they must bring Benjamin with them
When their food was exhausted again.

They said to each other, "We're being punished
For our treatment of Joseph way back,
And for telling our father that Joseph had perished."
How each conscience was on the rack!

Joseph spoke in Egyptian,
His brothers in the Hebrew tongue.
He turned away from them and wept,
As to each other they confessed
Their having done young Joseph wrong.
They did not know that their every word
He could understand,
For he spoke to them through an interpreter
Kept by him close at hand.

He commanded their sacks to be filled with corn,
The money they paid hid in each brother's sack,
And extra provisions he gave to sustain them
As to their father they travelled back.
At an inn one brother opened his sack,
For his ass, provender to provide.
He was stunned with startling amazement

When he found his money there inside.
Every brother's heart failed him
To find his money hid in his grain.
They asked each other if this was some punishment
Which upon them God had lain.

Ch. 43.

When Jacob heard their story,
He would not let Benjamin go
Until the food his sons had brought from Egypt
Was running very low.
Judah persuaded his father
From Benjamin briefly to sever,
Saying, "If I bring him not back again,
Mine be the blame for ever.
If we had not lingered, we would now be back
With a second life-saving store.
If we go not to Egypt with Benjamin,
He and us will soon be no more."

Judah must have been greatly relieved
To hear his father say,
"God grant you mercy before the man;
If I'm bereaved, I am bereaved."

To Egypt again the brothers returned.
Joseph saw that his wishes had not been spurned.

They were sent to his house;
A steward welcomed them in;
Joseph shed tears of joy on seeing Benjamin.
They told the steward of the money
They had each of them found in each sack.
The steward replied,
"The God of your father must have given it you back."
And as if to show that there was no problem,
He promptly gave Simeon back to them.

They gave to Joseph a present sweet:
They were given water to wash their feet.
To Joseph's house they were taken to dine;
Their asses too had it really fine.
Joseph asked of their father, "Is he alive and well?"
And was pleased with the tidings which they had to tell.
As they dined before him, arranged in order of birth,
They wondered that they were so arranged,
And yet they made merry, having such mirth.

Ch. 44.

Joseph ordered his steward,
"Fill the men's sacks with all they can hold;
But, before you seal it up,
Place in Benjamin's sack
My silver drinking and divining cup."
This incriminating enterprise
The steward efficiently organised,
And when the brothers had left the city
They were completely and unpleasantly surprised,
For after them speedily the friendly steward came,

To make them feel, although they were innocent,
An adopted sense of guilt and shame.

Back to Joseph they made their way.
Judah begged to be allowed
For the apparent offence to pay.
"No," said Joseph, "only he
Who had the cup shall be taken into custody."
Judah reminded Joseph of all he had heard before,
Offered himself as a slave
Benjamin's release to secure.
"I cannot return to my father," he said,
"I could not bear to hear his cry
And then to watch him suffering
And see him, heartbroken, die.

Ch. 45.

Thereupon, his emotions impossible to control,
Joseph ordered Egyptians to wait outside
While he told his brethren who he was;
That Joseph, their brother, had not died.
He asked them, "Does my father yet live?"
But none of his brethren an answer could give:
Every man struck dumb with fear,
Before mighty, much wronged Joseph thus to appear.

Joseph, anxious to allay their fear,
Bade his brothers to draw near,
And said, "The things I suffered at your hand

Were of God's will; by Him they were planned,
That in these times of famine dire
We might be preserved: both us, and our sire.
Now we must fetch him, while he lives and is well,
And in the land of Goshen you shall dwell.

Pharaoh himself was overjoyed.
All his resources he employed,
That Jacob might journey comfortably
To live in Goshen, beside the Great Sea.
Jacob suffered no indecision,
For God informed him in a vision,
His much loved son he there would see
And Israel would become a nation,
To stand for all futurity.

Ch. 46.

Travelling to Goshen, Jacob paused upon the way,
At memorable Beer-she-ba, his respects to God to pay.
He was rewarded with visions of the night,
In which God blessed the sojourn,
For it was planned by divine foresight.
Thus assured, Jacob rested content,
As onwards to Egypt his caravan went.

Seventy offspring of Jacob with him to Goshen went.
Two females only; his daughter and granddaughter,
Dinah and Serah, are named as present at this event.
One might otherwise have feared that Dinah

Had been held, as Prince Shechem,
To be as much to blame,
Was condemned, as was Tamar (later)
To die in judicial flame;
That she had paid that unthinkable penalty
Awarded to Tamar for Judah's hire,
But she was spared the fate which Tamar too avoided:
Her spark of life was not extinguished by fire.

Judah led to Goshen Jacob's caravan train.
Joseph in his chariot sped to see his sire again.
There, with great emotion, he wept, as was his style,
His face upon his father's neck and embracing for a while.
Jacob, having held his son and having him close by,
Said, "Now that I have seen your face,
In peace you may let me die."

Joseph warned his brothers,
"Shepherds here are abominated.
When Pharaoh asks your occupation,
Tell him you are cattlemen, if you would not be hated."

Ch. 47.

However, five of his brothers
To Pharaoh, "We are shepherds," declared;
But Joseph need not have worried,
For Pharaoh behaved as though he hadn't heard.

He summoned Joseph and told him,
"The land of Goshen is theirs."
Joseph must have heaved a sigh of relief:
He'd had less trouble ruling Egypt
Than running his family's affairs.

Pharaoh, interviewing Jacob,
Asked him how long a life he'd had.
Jacob answered, "I'm one hundred and thirty.
Few have been the years and bad."
Then he blessed Pharaoh and left him,
Perhaps feeling somewhat sad.

Joseph bought, in Pharaoh's name, everything in Egypt,
That to preserve the people
He would the better be equipped.
Lands and cattles, goods and chattels,
The people of Egypt themselves he bought,
That in the time of greatest need
From him their sustenance they sought.
And when to him, in need, they cried,
With fairness he their needs supplied.

There in the land of Egypt,
Seventeen more years Joseph knew.
During that time
The nation of Israel developed much
And in number grew.

When the time came that Jacob, as we all, must die,
He called his son, Joseph, to him saying,
"Place your hand under my thigh.
Deal kindly with me," he requested his son.
"Give me your oath, and to it be true,
That when you return to Canaan
My remains shall go with you."
Joseph swore the oath
That, when to Canaan their steps they retrace,
Jacob on dying will rest in Machpelah –
Abraham's and Isaac's long-purchased burial place.

Ch. 48.

Joseph heard that his father was sick
And with his sons, Manasseh and Ephraim,
To his father's bed he came.
Jacob summoned up his strength,
On his bed a sitting position to gain,
That he might to the trio
God's promises once more explain.
He blessed the younger son as greater than his brother,
And although Joseph protested emphatically
Jacob would do no other;
For, as a prophet, he could clearly see
The boy's descendants would bear their names
As tribes of Israel eternally.

Ch. 49.

Jacob on his deathbed appraised his sons.
Reuben, Simeon and Levi
Are described as unworthy ones.
Judah he identified as the one
Whom his brethren shall praise.
Zebulun by the sea shall dwell,
A haven for peaceful ways.
Issachar shall work with strength,
But will learn to appreciate rest.
Dan shall be a judge to his people,
But as such will be a pest.
Gad shall be beaten in warfare,
But will be victorious at last.
Asher shall be rich in food:
Every meal a repast.
Naphtali is a hind let loose.
Excellent his speech,
Universal and to eternity
Joseph's blessings shall reach.
Benjamin, as a wolf, shall ravin;
Early he shall devour his prey.
At night, he will divide the spoil
He won throughout the day.
Jacob, throughout the discourse,
Showed his love of righteousness.
The evil-doers he reproved,
The meritorious he did bless.
Upon the future he threw great light:
The Messiah Himself was in his sight.

Ch. 50.

Joseph had Jacob's body embalmed,
Which needed forty days.
Seventy were the days they mourned
To comply with Egyptian ways.
To remove Jacob's body from Egypt,
Pharaoh's permission was given.
Distinguished Egyptians were in the cortège;
In the finest vehicles, the mourners all were driven.
When Canaanites beheld the mourning
In the floor of Ated,
They changed its name to Abelmizraim*.
Empathising with the sad
And showing respect for the dead,
Seven more days to mourning they gave,
Then made their way across the Jordan,
Travelling on to bury Jacob in Machpelah's cave.

The family returned to Egypt,
Four hundred years, as a people, there to dwell.
Joseph's brethren, having lost their father,
Feared then that all would not be well.
They made up the tale that their father had said
That Joseph should take no revenge on them
When he was dead.
Joseph reminded his brothers
That he perfectly understood
That what they did was evil,
But God had meant it for good;

*Abelmizraim = Mourning of Egypt.

That many people should be kept alive
And Israel continue to thrive.

Joseph promised them love and care,
Which he maintained until he died.
Still with his family in Egypt there,
On his deathbed he made them swear:
When Israel depart to the Promised Land,
His remains away with them they would bear.
At one hundred and ten, all fears being calmed,
Joseph died and, for four hundred years,
In Egypt he lay embalmed.